THE HUNT
IN THE FOREST

POETRY
The Hoop
Common Knowledge
Feast Days
The Myth of the Twin
Swimming in the Flood
A Normal Skin
The Asylum Dance
The Light Trap
The Good Neighbour
Selected Poems
Gift Songs

FICTION
The Dumb House
The Mercy Boys
Burning Elvis
The Locust Room
Living Nowhere
The Devil's Footprints
Glister

NON-FICTION
A Lie About My Father

THE HUNT
IN THE FOREST

John Burnside

CAPE POETRY

Published by Jonathan Cape 2009

2 4 6 8 10 9 7 5 3 1

First published in Great Britain in 2009 by
Jonathan Cape
Random House, 20 Vauxhall Bridge Road,
London SW1V 2SA
www.rbooks.co.uk

Addresses for companies within The Random House Group Limited can be
found at: www.randomhouse.co.uk/offices.htm

The Random House Group Limited Reg. No. 954009

A CIP catalogue record for this book
is available from the British Library

ISBN 9780224089272

The Random House Group Limited supports The Forest Stewardship
Council (FSC), the leading international forest certification organisation.
All our titles that are printed on Greenpeace approved FSC certified paper
carry the FSC logo. Our paper procurement policy can be
found at www.rbooks.co.uk/environment

Mixed Sources
Product group from well-managed
forests and other controlled sources
www.fsc.org Cert no. TT-COC-2139
© 1996 Forest Stewardship Council

Typeset in Bembo by Palimpsest Book Production Limited,
Grangemouth, Stirlingshire

Printed and bound in Great Britain by
MPG Books Ltd, Bodmin, Cornwall

For Sarah, Lucas and Gil

Aimer la vérité signifie supporter le vide, et par suite accepter la mort. La vérité est du côté de la mort.
Simone Weil, *La pesanteur et la grâce*

What say you, gentlemen, shall we have a moonlight hunt?
R. L. Stevenson, *The Master of Ballantrae*

CONTENTS

LEARNING TO SWIM

All of a sudden and mostly by surprise
was how my cousin thought it should be done,
the body unlearning its weight as it plunged to the black
of the deep end and came, at a stroke,
to the friendship of water.

Older than me, and stronger, the playground tough,
he was quick with his hands and quicker still with his
     tongue,
but even he took a scare, that afternoon
in the public baths, when I didn't come up for so long,
lost in the blur of the pool as he stood at the rim,

trying to seem unconcerned, but numb with the fear
that he'd killed me, the glare of his laughter
dying away in the hollows and nooks of the roof
and everything silent: the lifeguard, the swoop of a diver,
the sky in the picture-windows, naked and cold.

Now, when I swim, I remember what failed to happen:
the body I never found in the glimmer of chlorine,
the casual ascent and the gleam of my cousin's approval;
I dream of the absence I missed and the shiver of longing
that played on my skin for as long as it took me to
     surface;

but what I remember best is the water's answer,
the shadow it left in my blood when it let me go
and the tug in my bones that remained, like a scar, or an
     echo,
concealing the death I had lost, but would cherish for
     years
as we cherish the faces of school-friends who never grow
     old.

THE HUNT IN THE FOREST

How children think of death is how the shadows
gather between the trees: a hiding place
for everything the grown-ups cannot name.
Nevertheless, they hurry to keep their appointment
far in the woods, at the meeting of parallel lines,
where everything is altered by its own
momentum – altered, though we say transformed –
greyhound to roebuck, laughter to skin and bone;

and no one survives the hunt: though the men return
in threes and fours, their faces blank with cold,
they never quite arrive at what they seem,
leaving a turn of phrase or a song from childhood
deep in the forest, bent to the juddering kill
and waiting, while their knives slip through the blood
like butter, or silk, until the heart is still.

IN MEMORIAM

I just hate to be a thing
Marilyn Monroe

I À BOUT DE SOUFFLE

Someone might call it ether, but for you
the light at the end of the tunnel is never quite air,

and breath is a shape that sails out over the rooftops,
into the lights off the quay and the tethered yawls.

Awake all night, as the lovers are awake
in that Godard film where everyone runs forever,

I think of you as fog, or phosphorescence
vanishing into the weft of the hospital linen,
b.p. and oxygen falling, like notes on a scale,

less song, than resonance, less cry, than chime:
a leyline in a field of iron filings,
or how a lost room settles in the bone,

pale as the fire in those cradles of horsehair and tallow
we used to burn out at the saltpans on wet afternoons,

coorying in like ghosts to the gold of the flame
and finding a home there – delicate; incomplete;

and perfect, like the grayscale in this film
that sifts out your future and seals it, in cirrus, then stone.

You never much cared for the angels
walking their finery home in a borrowed light,

ventriloquist, formal,
drenched in the distance of heaven;

but somewhere in the dark, beyond the rain,
crossing a meadow, or bent to a flickering kill,

the animal that matched you, note for note,
would catch a scent and turn, or lift its head

to listen, while this drizzle in the bone
pursued its course.
                      All night, on the surgery ward,

you were still playing catch on that strip
of lamplight and grass between home and the rest of the
    world,

the first rain turning to sleet
on the pavements and hedges,

the dog in your neighbour's garden
barking at no one;

or else, you were leaning in to the flicker and twitch
of a dream you could never enter, hoping to catch

the ghost of something feral in a slick
of dew
        or a ribbon of blood on a moonlit track

like the perfume of transit: that no man's land you find
on the drive to the airport, say, or a Sunday excursion:

a frontier of trees, or a pond at the edge of a meadow
where something you must have disturbed has hurried aside

and left you a liverish stain in the yellowing grass,
all feathers and teeth, and a tatter of hallelujah.

III WHEN THE MIND IS LIKE A HALL IN WHICH THOUGHT
      IS LIKE A VOICE SPEAKING, THE VOICE IS ALWAYS THAT
      OF SOMEONE ELSE

In the clinic it comes again
                    (*of being a thing*)

like stealing away to that mare's-nest of matchwood and straw
in the scullery
              – seven years old
and determined that nothing should perish –

                              illumined bone
immersed in the *noir*
of x-ray
        selvedge and skein
deciphered in the scan, until it seems

your body is a gloss
on something else:

a secret creature cradled in the skin
feeding on pain and sweetness

                    (*eldritch; angelic*)

a straggle of beak and feathers;
                        an arm's length of gristle

                    ★

– and then you are finding it
everywhere
              wood pigeons
                        lavender
rainwater pooled in a stump
of sycamore
            God
in the details

            perhaps

and perhaps
the geometry of one thing
then another.

Watching for spring
and the first warmth blown through the gorse
on the road to the graveyard
                              blisters of bud
and skin
            (*and that knot in the bone*)
uncurling
            (*how the flesh betrays itself*
is something to be observed
and then forgotten)

                        say these blossoms in the rain
are tokens for the heart
                        if not the hand

countering loss with surrender
                              decay with gain
– bloodroot and campion; clutches of thrift and narcissus –

this evidence you found
                        then found again
rephrasing the heart
in a ravel of swansdown and webbing.

                              ★

A paradise of birds
in a wash of static:

finch in the bones
of the hand, or the smaller falcons;

curlew and harrier, godwit
and sacred ibis.

Or here, what remains
of iguana, or axolotl,

sung from the cloud
of a body that never felt

as solid as it looked:
interiors

of maidenhair and fog where,
every night,

the hunter seeks its prey
– the gone to ground

of something in the heart
you cannot name,

after the pigsqueal and judder
of untold love.

★

In the stories they used to tell
on mornings like this,
a boy and his sister would walk out into the dark
and never return;

or someone would find a knife
in a wave of ash
and cut the line that bound him to this world,
a locked sleep bobbing away in the April wind.

How suddenly, it seems, the house falls still,
even the owls have stopped in the nether field,
and the cars on the coast road
blur into wind and distance;

yet all night the stories return
in altered form:
a marriage falling open like a book
and sloe-coloured insects spilling across the floor;

or, from the walls, an interrupted sound,
like someone thinking, in an empty hall,
from thought to song, from song to widowhood,
a voice that is quiet and clear, till you open the door.

In the stories they used to tell
for the soon-to-be-dead
a woman comes in from the garden
shaking the snow from her coat in a lighted hall,

the lamp on the kitchen table a stored
Magnificat,
the vase of poppy-heads and winter sweet
suspended, like a missed Annunciation

and, caught in the perfect lull
between lost and found,
her body becomes
a footnote to itself,

light as a feather, blood-warm,
utterly whole
and dry as the voice her grandmother kept in reserve
for love songs and premonitions

★

– and that's how it must have been, when the daylight
thickened and stalled on your hands
and you put down the book you were reading
to listen;
          no angel, of course,

but you turned to the window, lightened with
     expectation,
and something was there, after all: the smell off the
     meadows,
the last sun pooled
in the beech-hedge and, further away,

9

the dog-fox from down in the valley, come up to
　　hunt
for mice, in the first days of harvest, everything
dusted with sugar and flame, from your bed to the
　　shore
and beyond
　　　　　and out on the road

a grey wind in from the sea to gather you home:
no sign of the angel, no word, no Annunciation,
only the cool of it, finding your lips and fingers
and burrowing in, for the sweetness that darkens the
　　bone.

FETCH

Like a summer of fog and midges
come overnight

to wrap you, bone by bone,
in its yellowing velvet,

she finds you at three in the morning
brushing your hair,

and that shudder and dunt at the pier
is the ferry arriving:

                    leaf-smoke
and last year's harvest

spread on the deck like a fishnet
and just the occasional

shimmer and thrash to show
for what tipped the scale

from sugar and malt
to the silver of nothing but.

RICH

He could carry a swarm of bees to the edge of a meadow
and set it down,

or sit in the parlour till dark with his grandfather's bible,
reading Galatians or Acts while the lights of the village

quickened then faded without him, the church halls and
    taprooms
filling with music and barter, the shops closing up

on dry goods, white goods,
liquorice in jars.

On nights when he didn't sleep, he lay awake
in happiness:

a dream he had built from the pallor of 50s snapshots,
faces like cornfields or acres of matinee snow,

the last days of summer or childhood reduced over years
to biscuit ware and alstroemeria,

the same birthdays over and over, the same premonitions,
abandoned bowls of lemonade and rain,

and every day his life would start anew,
simple and incomplete, like those old-fashioned songs

that came on the wireless at teatime, his mother and sister
singing along as the back door opened and closed

on flaked corn and apples, on pine-tar and blackstrap molasses
and field after field of names, to the ends of the earth.

NIGHT SHIFT AT THE PLUG MILL

Four hours into the dark I'd fall asleep
for seconds, then wake to the scream
of gears, as the belt started up
and the formed tubes dropped to the rack,
still bright from the fire:

sometimes I had to step in over the teeth
with a crowbar and straighten them out,
the heat flowing back through my arms and into my
     heart,
the rack shifting under my feet, while I bobbed and
     swayed
and watched for the misalignment that might kill me;

and sometimes the wheels turned smoothly all night
     long
while I sat in the cabin and gazed off into the lights
of the freight yard, where trains slid by

like the trains in a film about wartime or mass
     transportation,
fresh snow drifting in waves between brickwork and
     gables
or standing an hour at the door, till it came to
     nothing.

AN ESSAY CONCERNING LIGHT

*O nobly-born, listen. Now thou art experiencing the Radiance
of the Clear Light of Pure Reality. Recognize it. O nobly-born,
thy present intellect, in real nature void, not formed into anything
as regards characteristics or colour, naturally void, is the very
Reality, the All-Good.*

The Tibetan Book of the Dead (tr. W.Y. Evans–Wentz)

I SCOTLANDWELL

All summer long, I waited for the night
to drive out in the unexpected gold
of beech woods, and those lighted homesteads, set
like kindling in the crease-lines of the dark,

catching a glimpse, from the road, of huddled dogs
and sleepless cattle, mustered in a yard
as one flesh, heads
like lanterns, swaying, full of muddled light;

light from the houses television blue,
a constant flicker, like the run of thought
that keeps us from ourselves, although it seems
to kindle us, and make us plausible,

creatures of habit, ready to click
into motion. All summer long,
I knew it had something to do
with looking again, how something behind the light

had gone unnoticed; how the bloom on things
is always visible, a muddled patina
of age and colour, twinned with light or shade
and hiding the source of itself, in its drowned familiar.

By the time there is nothing to shed
there is something to gather,

the new life catching its breath
and kicking in,

no more substantial, at first,
than the promise of snow,

but a darkening, nevertheless,
in the fabric of light

where everything unmade
begins again.

Hard to imagine a last voice fading away
when the brightness opens

and not admire a system where the dead
go singly towards the light – and with such good grace –

adding, or taking away,
from here, or forever,

no more than a random droplet
of morning rain

adds to the river: a far cry
and scarcely a ripple.

On some days it feels like a gift,
flaws in the line of a sumac becoming

linnets, or finches,
strayed from a roadside verge,

the cat from the nearby farm
picked out, where its body remembers

stalking
        – on days like this,
late in July, the night heat shaping itself

to a body I might have possessed,
had I learned before now

how empty it was
              and how ready
to enter the light.

All afternoon
there was something alive in the hedge

– a blackbird, I thought, or a thrush;
though nothing sang –

while the cow fell, then got to her feet,
only to fall again, her hind-legs

collapsing under the weight, as we tried
to set her right: her mad eyes

staring – though not at us, who were
irrelevant
        distracting her from what she almost

saw behind us, looming like the dusk
of someone else's day, not hers, or ours,

a darkening
that still might be transformed

to music in the hedge: blackbird, or thrush,
returning from the light, to claim its own.

As children we thought it meant
what it seemed to say,

as if two cities stood on either bank
of one enormous river,

the first overcrowded, busy with trade
and betrayal,

the second pared down
to essentials: a clouded bazaar,

a boy on his way to church
in the midsummer heat,

and someone in a kitchen, eating
pomegranates, while the wakeful dead

wandered away, through side streets
and dusty squares,

with all they could carry: a fish-knife,
a string of pearls,

a story, begun in childhood,
or halfway through marriage,

the one thing they should have
completed, the light everlasting,

passing from one to the next
in a cradle of skin.

There are those who say we can choose,
when the moment comes:

a shape stealing home from the woods, a loping fox,
or the smallest of birds, come in through an open

window
        – firecrest, or wren –
a flutter against the wall, or a ribbon of music;

and, sometimes, a friend or a lover,
twenty years on,

the old hurts dissolved,
ambivalence forgotten.

Me, I would take the back road, out by the loch:
a moorhen in the reeds, the flush of dawn,

and no-one behind me, calling, again and again,
go into the light
            nobly-born
                go into the light.

STALKERS

Tell me again
the stories you tell a child

when the season begins
and the hunters are out on the moor,

daylong, out in the rain
and the fabric of air.

How everything
is governed by a law:

the creatures we use
and the creatures

we cannot imagine.
How nothing can be concealed

forever: not the hexagrams
of scent

    and not
the milk and honey shadow

of the stalker,
when he steps into the veil,

and something comes to meet him
on the wind,

fallow and cold

    and sweet,
like the mouth of his bride.

AMOR VINCIT OMNIA

The one thing that no one would choose
and it's back, like a knife at a wedding:

child's play, a half mile of rail tracks
and four steps into the woods, the abandoned shoes

laid out for keeps
in a chamber of ground frost and ticking.

The creatures dissolve in the grass
like ribbons of gunsmoke

and all that remains of the day is a sodden
fallow, like the pallor in the eyes

of something held, then
casually discarded.

Between the trees,
all miles-to-go and kindling,

pine needles, larch bones,
siftings of bootblack and smocking;

a few steps more, and the ground goes
from under your feet:

a vault of chalk and hair, laid down for years
to draw you in: a slumber; then a waking.

WINTER

Imagine I loved you still and nights like these
were visitations,
an endless Pentecost of lips and hands
and bodies resurrected in their beds,
not mine, or yours, but given, like a snowfall.

Out in the dark, the woods are from a map
that someone has left unfinished: hand-coloured signs
for birch, or deer, and nothing to explain
the new red of a kill, or how the silence
wells around a fallen sycamore;

but here, where we lie down in differing weather,
the night fades on our skins while we are dreaming,
and winter is the self, day after day,
ghosting a life from the nothing it knows by heart.

ECHO ROOM

All night, the long-eared bats
flicker from tree to tree
through the scent of rain;

the luckiest survive for fifteen years,
quick, in the swim of the air
or skimming the earth

where cats from the village
pluck them entire from the darkness.

To the Ancient Chinese
they meant luck;
to the Flemish, affection;

but, here, what they most resemble
is desire:

all skitter and echo,
gathering, then forgetting.

THE SYMPOSIUM

We would creep to an upstairs room
at the end of the party,
or wander out into the garden,
to lie down in a wave of trees and stars,

but mostly what we wanted was to find
the creatures we'd known before, in some earlier life,
touching again, to suffer the recognition,
the mineral sweetness – copper, or verdigris –
veining what we took to be the soul.

It's not what we remember is the echo,
but all the things forgotten: mist and stone,
light in the grass, then wind, then nothingness,
the music distance makes and, at the last,
the sudden chill that trickles through our hands.

DOCUMENTARY

I keep imagining another place:

somewhere from one of those slightly too plausible films
where the street is a parallel street in a parallel world

and everything altered slightly, though not that much,
only another version of what we know

going about its business, our parallel selves
brighter and more successful than we seem,

but touched, still, with a possibility:
the parallel, we're led to guess,

of *us*.
    So it continues, one world feeding the next
with minor variations, like the days

we pass so calmly, unaware of all this
business: quarks

and singularities,
and everything coming to light in a fold of time

where something that never was, or might have been,
occurs, at last, in some infinity,

to people much like us, though not quite us,
who think of us more fondly than we know.

RAIN

And thou shalt renew the face of the earth
The Office of the Holy Spirit

On certain nights, when everyone is sleeping,
I drive out into the meadows to watch the bats,
alone in the car, with the windows all the way down
for the cool of the air and the quiet beyond the
    village;

moths in the grass and the bats dipping out of the
    trees,
slipping from lit to dark, from unseen to seen,
in the waver of headlamps, all wingbeat and blur in
    the chill
that comes, after hours of rain, from the still of the
    woods

and the hollows of cat-hair and stone in old
    farmsteads and mills
where the dead are no longer sleeping, or lying
    awake,
though the spirit is creeping, inchwise, through
    mortar and blood,
unpicking the fabric, renewing the face of the earth.

KAPELLØYA

Wonders will never
cease.
      In the yellow of dawn

she took up her garment
of pain
        and nostalgia for pain

and set herself down on the rocks
to recover a world:

wind in her face
and a skitter of bone in the tide

as she worried the stone
with her hands
          till the fingers

bled;
    yet
day after day,

with gratitude,
alone,

she lowered her head
to the ground
        as if in defeat

or refusal
      numb to the roll
of the sea
       and the shifting

gravity of kittiwake
and herring.

After a week,
the rock was as smooth and as clear

as glass
　　　and she hunkered down
to gaze on the stubborn fact

of matter
　　　the fathomless
blue of it
　　　latticed and veined

and foxed
　　　like the dreaming
flesh in an old

anatomy.

Later
　　the people came
from the village
　　　or crossed

from the mainland
　　　a score of hands

to set against
the blindness in the stone

– mothers and children,
fisherfolk, curious tourists –

come for the backward glance
as it turns to salt

or the flicker of ash and guile
in the still of the land

where everything they thought
was gone to dust

is gathered in
　　　and harrowed
for safe keeping.

THE SECRET LIFE OF
PORNOGRAPHY

There might be another room
at the back of the house

where a boyhood of gauze and linnets
is laid out in drawers,

numbered and pinned
like the baize in a county museum;

but no one here will speak about *the soul*,
only the puppets and clocks at the local

flea market: gaps
for abandon and home, to be measured and occupied later,

after a *carnevale* of crumpled silk
and peaches – and that girl you never knew

making that sound you had heard of
but couldn't have hoped for

over and over
and never quite reaching the end

till the child in you parleys
for wishbones and mother love.

POPPY DAY

The butcher arrives with a love song
he learned from his father.

Out on the kill floor, veiled in a butterslick
circumflex of marrowfat and bone,
he rinses off the knife and goes to work,
his voice so sweet, the children come to hear

the beauty of it, slipped between a vein
and what the veal calf thought would last
forever.
      Barely a shudder rises through the hand
that holds the blade
                and yet he guides it down
so gently, it falls open, like a flower.

And still the children come, to hear him sing,
his voice so soft, it's no more than a whisper.

ULEY BLUE

I found a badger
struck down in the road,

as if by some
misgiving.

Tatters of blue
in the face, though not

the blue of woad
or of that stream

in Gloucestershire,
where young girls would

have put away their work
to watch the huntsmen

pass,
blue as the sky.

From some old
courtesy, I

dragged the body up
on to the verge,

then stood a while
as if to see it

blunder away
to the cloud-blue

of oat grass
and brambles,

but something in it,
stubborn as a wave,

refused that resurrection
while the rain

came slow and steady,
ink spots in the dust

and something like a hand
smoothing the fur

from blue, to grey,
and then to black and white.

TRAPPIST

This morning has the air of hospice flowers,
scents that seem newly invented, and here for a reason,
damp pinks and pioneer blues, from the age
of Kodachrome;

but the questions are always the same, like the questions
    we ask
of still life: why the open door appears
to bring the garden in and sit it down
between the kitchen and the empty hall,

or how it seems a death has been rehearsed
only a moment since: the threshold glazed
with silence, like the silence in a play
when somebody misses his cue, or forgets his lines
and stands gazing out at the lights
till he hears the prompt

*

or that one afternoon in the year
when something like a distance in the woods
wanders across the garden and steps indoors,
touched with the midsummer heat
and the scent of blossom;

never the ghost you expected, but someone familiar,
a man your age, perhaps, with the hint of a smile
you remember from somewhere else: all
angles, but light as a feather,
and nothing to show for the journey from nowhere to here.

Not what you hoped for: no answer, no transformation,
only a man your age, like your father before you,
standing alone in the hallway, your father's father,
sober for once, and lucky to be alive,
your grandfather's father, that grammar of distance and
    blood.

THE VISITOR

I sometimes expected the Visitor who never comes.
                                    Thoreau

No one is crossing the yard
this April morning.
Small rain fuzzes the light
from the kitchen door
and the dog shape that worried the fence line
flickers away through the grass
to the last grey of dawn.

Half a mile up the road
my neighbour's orchard
falls through the gentian darkness like a word
unspoken.
       No one is walking home
from the nether field
cradling a lamb in his arms, or singing a hymn
he's surprised to remember

and no one is here, by the gate,
with a song in his head,
some tune from the gnosis of love
in the last days of childhood,
coming to light like a wish
or the nub of a tumour.

THE MISSING

Like one of those friendships I always intended to have
and never quite managed, distracted by other things

– family, schoolwork, that roundness the self acquires
on quiet days, surrounded by its few

possessions;
        like the kin I never had,
there was always an echo, waiting to be recovered,

something to do with sports days, or Midnight Mass,
the handling of money, the milk-scent and swim of the future.

Somebody died.
        It was one of the neighbours, I think:
the woman who stood at her door in a polka-dot dress

and gazed off along the street, as if she were
waiting for someone to come

from the pits, or the distance,
the boy who climbed the fence at St Columba's

and hung on a spike, till a slaughterman ran from the yards
and hoisted him off,

or maybe the Polish girl from the next street along,
sent to bed early one night
        and gone in the morning:

somebody died
        and the others were left behind
so that I could save them;

but nobody answered by name
when I called the rolls,

busy, as everyone is, with something else:
a light they might enter, the green of a world to come.

AN ESSAY CONCERNING TIME

Only the dead are communal:
intimate under the grass, conversing through snow,
forever gifted with the middle ground,

only the dead are immune
to clockwork,
in its sleeve of zinc and lime.

Lying awake, they slide beneath the blades
and, though they see us, when we light our fires
at daybreak,

        though they know us through our songs
and customs,
        they are leaving us behind,

released from this local need
to manage time,
passing through aeons as if they were long afternoons

and coming home to what they cannot lose:
gulls in the wake of a plough, like a bridal train
and the faces of children, lost in quadratic equations.

II VIEW TO THE WEST ACROSS THE VALLEY OF THE
WOUNDED KNEE BATTLEGROUND WITH SLAIN
AMERICAN DAKOTA SIOUX AND BURIAL PARTY
BARELY VISIBLE ABOVE COTTONWOODS ALONG THE
CREEK, PINE RIDGE RESERVATION, SOUTH DAKOTA,
DECEMBER 1890

It seems they might still be there
if we found the place:

ghost dancers peppered with snow
in the winter light,

their stitched shirts like a memory
of feathers, and that faded, hatchling gaze

in faces that would come to life again
if anything was there to be remembered.

Nothing is there; or only the middle ground
where deer had crossed and vanished years before,

the girlish bodies dimming, one by one,
as old men dimmed before the camera,

elders with names like gifts
or second lives,

forgetting, in a maze of light and glass
the brimming fields, the miles of buffalo.

The places we never visit:
the Shinto gates, the courtyards of sorted gravel,
the inward rooms of long-abandoned temples

sacred beyond our knowing;
                                          those old-stone
bridges in Königsberg, spanning the thought of a river,

a puzzle that no one can solve, though we guess
how it goes;

                    or that point, to the nearest second,
mid-afternoon,
when someone indoors looks up, and the window darkens,

not one thing after another, but both at once:
this knowledge we have that no one is truly absent,
and nothing is ever the same as the shape it resembles,

time like a room in the house
that no one can enter;

the watchmaker checking his clock, as the shadow moves on,
the man in his frock coat and gloves, on the cusp of forever.

*They kept not the covenant of God, and refused to walk in his law;
And forgat his works, and his wonders that he had shewed them.*

Psalms 78: 10-11

Who was it took a brush, a tin of paint,
a weathered blank of matchwood from a fence,
and spelled these letters out, to damn his kind,
a welter of shadows, hidden in plain sight?

Perhaps what passed for wisdom in his world
was this: a form of grief mixed with the names
of birds and grasses, how to set a bone
or cook a poultice
                              even when he knew

the shaping ailment lodges in the heart
– sin being what we have, and true to us
like nothing else, not brotherhood or wonder –
and God was lost, who never came for him

as world and pleasure came
to hold him down,
so nothing could go up, against that look
the sky becomes, when kinfolk are remembered.

Like going to meet a friend
in the abstract: that same
preparedness of heart;

though no one is there, at the last, in the quiet room
that so much resembles
the room you have just abandoned,

a dribble of paint on the threshold,
a coat hung to dry;

or that hut at the end of the track
that runs through the woods,

a space long-abandoned, all
potsherds and spidered jars.

Imagine it: a low roof and a stove,
a dozen books at most, some photographs,
long-ago pencils, stamp albums, childish loves

and a music that nobody hears, in the air of a door
left open for the taste of sand and pines.

Félix Vallotton: Le ballon, 1899

Golden inside, though only the moving parts
are honey; the rest

is walnut and paint-flakes, numbers engraved in dust,
the birdsong of foreign cities, where someone else

imagines a self from folk songs
and words from a missal;

golden, like the light that falls across
a knoll in the public gardens, where a child

in a straw hat and pinafore chases a red balloon
towards the trees,

her flight like the passing of time, or the end of a summer,
not to be interrupted, true

perfection, like the figures by the lake,
and not quite perfected in death, but passing away,

as everything passes, becoming itself in the shift
from here to there, from near to almost gone.

We move so easily from light to shade
and always in pursuit of something else:

not what we manage, not what we think we can hold
– the red balloon, perhaps,

                        the red and green

of summer in the morning, in the park –
but what the child pursues beyond herself,

knowing the limits of self, and the perfume of distance:
the nothing she would gather in her arms

bouncing away to forever,
and not for the taking.

AMOR VINCIT OMNIA

What we need now
is fog;

     fog, and the pincushion baize
of pine trees
          like the trees in Chinese paintings.

What we need now is distance and local tradition;
the *breve* of italic; the *minim* of untold love;

a new vocabulary
of now-or-never:

names for the things we have lost,
          so we know what to mourn.

HONEYBEE SUTRA

Here is another
witness: blood-warm
sift, and a quicksilver pulse,
drifting between the poles
of loosestrife and sorrel;
and isn't it the dead
we hope to find,
packed
in the dripping combs
like microfiche:
uncles and mothers
sauntering home in a glaze
of nectar and honey,
love in the blood like wax
and that gift
for navigation, gathered from a wisp
of thistledown?
All afternoon
they sway
through an empty house:
mothers and uncles,
grandfathers,
school friends,
wives,
finding the well of a jar
or the sky in a mirror,
waves of them
spun from the hive
of another
life.

AHIMSA BEE SUTRA

Doubtless, a place is reserved
at the end of the house
for woodlice and gnats,
for craneflies and death-watch beetle;

or else, behind the furthest rainslicked door
a yellow cupboard full of lice and moths
ticks like a heart, or a cloud,
in the kindly dark.

The house of the self, perhaps, with its sloping floors
and *trompe l'oeil,*
where, tonight, you will gather bees from the smoke
    and the noise,
heavy and dark, like a bundle of stonewashed linen.

Heavy and dark, like embers, or last year's flood,
they will tumble in golden rolls from the flyblown
    hide
of a lion: rooms of honey in the bones,
the mane a haze of crimson and forgetting

and, all the while, the unconsidered slide
of rise and fall, of one thing, then another:
that broken space behind the lion's eye
another swarm; this hive, a resurrection.

TREATISE ON THE VEIL

alles aarzelt
voor het Definitieve
Roland Jooris

I AUGUST

Pewits over the fields
all afternoon

and the day too cold
for summer:
           that shade of grey

you know from Super-8
or Danish painting

slipping in along the fence-wires rimmed
with water and grime
                the whelk-blue

and mother-of-pearl
of swollen ditches on the Lochty road

catching the sky
in a long blear of slurry and diesel.

Not quite night
but the shadow is out in the grass

and the darkness that stands in the window
to draw you home

is the first day of late middle-age
as you drift indoors

45

and sit for an hour in the kitchen
before going up

to lie down with the last remaining
vestige of the bride
                            her powdered veils

falling across your face
and the scent of vixen

blurring your fingers and mouth
as you try for the grace

of something that used to be yours
in the not yet given.

If happiness is how you think of time

– as salt and crimson, say,
or sudden fog

arriving at the door and peering in
like someone come to ask

about a kitten –

then love must be the white in which you bury
everything you cannot bear away,

the puzzlement of cattle, staring back
across a sodden gatepost, or the stranger's

lipstick on a cup, mid-afternoon,

when you're halfway through washing up
and alone for a lifetime.

III THE DEFINITIVE

There will, no doubt, be signs
and sudden voices:

lines in a spill of flour
and a covey of schoolgirls

passing the window
or calling across the park.

Autumn by then,
of course; those early shades

of butternut and rust, of rose
and green,

and already a hint of rock-salt
under the leaves,

though nothing like the shortfall
you expected:

snow, when it comes,
that gap at the back of the mind

where time is neither
measure nor acquittal,

only the intricate hunger
of what would replace you:

the cool at your neck
when you turn round and no one is watching,

the bruise in the gaslight
where something remains to be born.

AMOR VINCIT OMNIA

Find me when summer ends and the lamps
are everything.

I have practised being the one
to whom you return,

if not the betrothed, then at least
the autumnal familiar,

the almost unveiled.

Songlike and lost in the mist, I have made you a bed
of fingerprints and outlook and those

footsteps that go in the dark
through a litmus of snow

to seek benediction.

Call it a house of cards,
or a hall of mirrors,

but nothing will measure you here
and find you wanting.

SAINT HUBERT AND THE DEER

He has come to a halt in the woods:
snow on the path
               and everything gone to ground
in its silken lair;

gone to ground
           or folded in a death
so quiet, he can almost taste the fade
of hair and vein,

the flesh gone into light
and water
       part-song
           lost in all this glitter.

Nothing is less attractive than the heart,
but we have to admire
its utter disdain for comfort.

Nothing is so relentless or intact
and death is its only precision:
               at the last
a voice will form beyond the empty trees

and something will glimmer away
               to the far edge of vision,
the deer, perhaps:

       the deer,
          but not the prey
he sought for years
       and cannot bear to master.

OLD MAN, SWIMMING

When I was twenty years old, on days that were
darker and brighter than now,
I got up at six and swam fifty lengths every morning,

steady and even, though not as precise, or as sure
as the one other swimmer I passed, flowing back and
    forth,
in the lit pool on Parker's Piece:

an old man, I thought at the time,
with a gold to his skin
that is only acquired over decades, his slicked hair

silver, his bachelor's eyes
halfway from grey to blue, when we met
in the changing rooms, silent and male,

but never so much that it bothered him not to
    conceal
a fleeting, and half-amused gleam
of fellow feeling.

He was my model for years,
with his gorgeous stroke
and his lack of determination,

something that looked like happiness
pushing him on
for mile after mile of easy, unnumbered laps

and I wanted to be like that,
but I never got past
the effort, the mental arithmetic, the thoughts

of later, or somewhere else
– though, at the time,
I put it down to age, experience,

an old man's gift for knowing how much he could
    do,
and it's taken till now to see that he wasn't so old,
just graceful, and lit with the years

he had carried so far:
the same age as I am today, more or less,
as I pass the municipal baths in another town

and glance across the blue-grey of the park
to where the better self I meant to be
glides quietly, length by length, to his own abstention.

ACKNOWLEDGEMENTS

Acknowledgments are due to the editors of the following:

The Financial Times, *Granta*, *London Review of Books*, *Poetry Review* and *The Times Literary Supplement*.

The sequence 'In Memoriam' was commissioned by the Edinburgh International Book Festival.

The poem 'Kapelløya' was prompted by a work by Martine Linge, created as part of Genius Loci in Vest-Agder, 2002.